The
LITTLE BOOK
of
CHRISTMAS
and
HOGMANAY

The LITTLE BOOK of CHRISTMAS and HOGMANAY

Scotland's Festive Traditions

Anna Marshall

BIRLINN

First published in 2025 by
Birlinn Limited
West Newington House
10 Newington Road
Edinburgh
EH9 1QS

www.birlinn.co.uk

ISBN 978 1 78027 960 2

*British Library Cataloguing
in Publication Data*
A catalogue record for this book is
available from the British Library.

Designed and typeset by
Mark Blackadder

Papers used by Birlinn Ltd are
from well-managed forests and
other responsible sources

Printed and bound by
Bell & Bain Ltd, Glasgow

Contents

Scottish Festive Timeline

1583   Scottish Presbyterian Church bans Christmas celebrations

1600   Oldest known reference to Christmas Day football game

1640   Act of Parliament makes celebrating Christmas illegal

1650   First record of the Kirkwall Ba' Game

1752   Scotland adopts the Gregorian Calendar and Christmas moves forward 11 days

1788   Robert Burns writes 'Auld Lang Syne'

1841   First festive card printed

1852   First mention of Santa in a British newspaper

1862   'Deck the Halls' written

1872   First Edinburgh–Glasgow Rugby Derby

1881   First official Up Helly Aa festival

1891   First selfie Christmas card created

1939	The Broons first annual published
1939–45	Hogmanay Fire festivals banned due to wartime blackout restrictions
1947	First Norwegian Christmas Tree on the Mound, Edinburgh
1958	Christmas becomes a public holiday
1967	Christmas tree imports to Shetland banned due to foot-and-mouth
1971	Christmas Day and Boxing Day declared Bank Holidays
1976	Stanley Baxter's *Christmas Box* airs
1987	First Loony Dook
1995	Snowiest Christmas on record
2000	First *Chewin' the Fat* Hogmanay Special
2017	Stromness Log Pull tradition revived

Introduction

Many of the Christmas and New Year traditions that we enjoy in Scotland have a fascinating and complicated history. Long before there was a concept of Christmas, the people of Scotland were inventing ways to brighten the dark days of winter. Over 5,000 years ago, our ancient ancestors built Maeshowe in Orkney. They painstakingly positioned it to track the setting sun during the winter solstice, allowing them to pinpoint the long-awaited moment when the days started to lengthen.

Customs that we think of as intrinsically Christmassy have often emerged from a melting pot of influences and beliefs: the Celts had a rich culture of winter rituals; the Vikings brought us the pagan celebrations of Yule; the Romans introduced us to their festival of Saturnalia; and the spread of Christianity led to Scots celebrating the birth of Jesus Christ. All of these festivities feed into the traditions that we practice today.

Despite the richness of our wonderfully eclectic, amalgamated Christmas heritage, we very nearly lost Christmas entirely – frankly it is remarkable that we have retained any Christmas traditions at all. After the Reformation, Christmas was outlawed for nearly 400 years. This meant that for several centuries the focus of our winter celebrations shifted to New Year. Today we Scots love everything to do with Christmas, from the cheesiest tunes to the John Lewis adverts, but we retain a strong sense of the significance of New Year – or perhaps we still just like an excuse for a winter party.

As if banning Christmas didn't make our festive

traditions complicated enough, in the eighteenth century we shifted the date of Christmas and New Year forward by 11 days by changing from the Julian calendar to the Gregorian calendar. Not everyone was keen on this idea, and for decades many Scots stubbornly continued to celebrate 'Old Christmas' and 'Old New Year' 11 days later than the rest of the world, which makes the writing of any history of Scottish Christmas incredibly confusing.

This book is a joyous miscellany of Scotland's Christmas and Hogmanay customs. It is a *ceilidh* in book form – full of history, recipes, music, poetry and storytelling. Our traditions are creative, elaborate and sometimes bizarre. Some rituals are unique to tiny communities, like the Jarl Squad Brownie troop of Walls in Shetland; some are specific to certain regions, such as the practice of throwing fermented porridge at grumpy people in Aberdeenshire; and others are celebrated more widely, like our famous Hogmanay street parties. The range and variety of ways in which we celebrate Christmas and Hogmanay is staggering, and we add to our heritage by creating new traditions every year. In our fast-changing world we can't know what a Scottish Christmas will look like in the future, but judging by our history it can only get more extraordinary.

Yule

Yule was originally a pagan festival marking the winter solstice. It was celebrated primarily in Scandinavia, and the Vikings brought it to Scotland. Traditionally Yule would have been celebrated over several weeks, with great drinking and feasting.

Yule is still celebrated in some of Scotland's northern and island communities, particularly in Shetland. There they traditionally partied every night for three weeks while observing an elaborate host of feasts, superstitions and customs such as opening the front door on Christmas morning to let Yule in, setting a new broom by the door, wearing clean, new clothes and eating sun-shaped cakes to celebrate the lengthening of the days.

Trows

Some of the most unusual Yuletide beliefs relate to Scotland's most notorious mythical beings, trows. A trow is a goblin-like creature, sometimes referred to as a fairy. They are extremely mischievous, sometimes malevolent, characters that appear in many Scottish folktales.

Trows were believed to be most active during the Helly (Holy) days of Yule. During this time their magic was at its most powerful and they would venture above ground intent on causing trouble. People took serious steps to prevent the creatures from entering their homes. It was believed that a locked door would not stop a trow, but that a steel knife placed above the doorway would prevent them from entering your house. Similarly, crosses made of straw, talismans made of hairs from each of your livestock and lighted lamps were believed to repel the trows. Above all, trows were attracted by mess and loved to meddle with unfinished work. An unclean house enticed trows, as did spinning wheels and looms, which had to be dismantled and removed to an outbuilding.

Even pregnant women weren't spared the trows' mischief. During Yule expectant mothers were said to hear a gleeful warning that their babies would grow to be fitful and mournful – all because the trows had deliberately broken the holy days.

Ye ken a
green Yule
makes a fat
kirkyard.

Scottish proverb

Sowans

Sowans are a fermented drink made of oat husks that was traditionally drunk during Yule. Once the drink had been strained the leftover husks could also be made into a porridge. In Aberdeenshire, Christmas Eve was known as Sowans Night. Naughty children in North-east Scotland enjoyed throwing the porridge at the windows of *near-b'gyaun* (miserly, grumpy people).

INGREDIENTS

For the drink:
150g oatmeal
650ml water

For the porridge:
300ml water
1½ tbsp caster sugar
½ tbsp salt

METHOD

1. Place the oatmeal and water into a jar and mix well.
2. Cover the jar with cheesecloth or a tea towel and secure round the rim with an elastic band.
3. Leave the mixture to ferment for at least four days, stirring occasionally.
4. After four days smell the liquid, it should have a distinctive acidic tang. If not, leave it to ferment for another couple of days.
5. Strain the liquid through a fine sieve. This liquid can now be drunk as sowans.
6. To make the porridge, place the leftover oatmeal in a saucepan over a medium heat.
7. Add the water, sugar and salt.
8. Cook for 7–8 minutes, stirring until the mixture thickens.
9. Serve the porridge warm with honey and milk.

Bringing Greenery into the Home

Many hundreds of years before the advent of Christianity, Celtic people brought evergreen plants such as holly and ivy into their homes during the winter to ward off evil spirits. The practice has survived millennia of cultural and religious change. Even today many people unwittingly continue the traditions of their Celtic ancestors, often using winter greenery to decorate their fireplaces, dinner tables and bannisters.

There is however one type of winter greenery that is unlikely to have been part of the ancient Celtic customs. Mistletoe has been a popular feature of Christmas since the mid-nineteenth century, but although there are over 1,500 varieties of mistletoe, there is only one that grows in Britain, and it is usually concentrated in areas of south-east England. It is only very rarely seen in Scotland. The mistletoe that you might buy while choosing your Christmas tree has most likely been imported from Europe. But all that may be about to change. There have recently been reports of an explosive spread of mistletoe across Britain, possibly due to climate change and deviation in migratory bird behaviour. Perhaps we'll see locally-grown Scottish mistletoe yet.

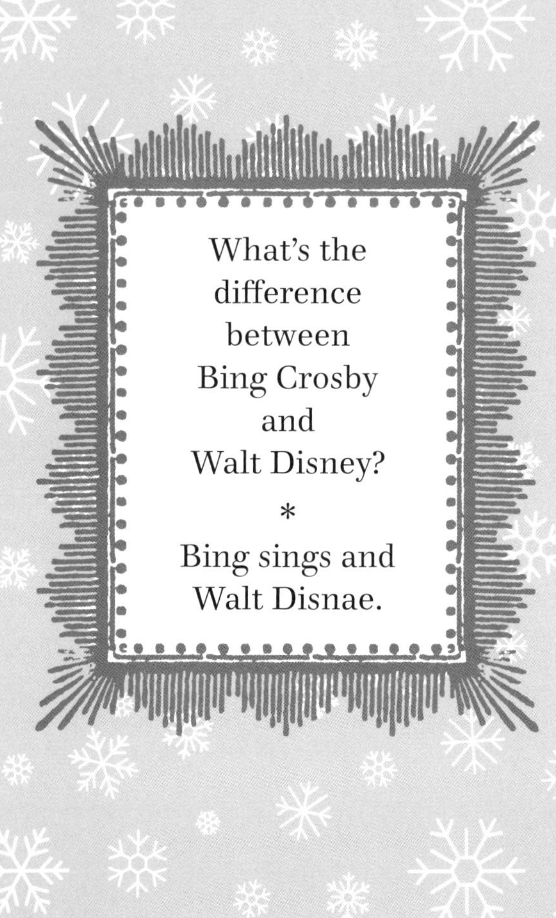
What's the
difference
between
Bing Crosby
and
Walt Disney?

*

Bing sings and
Walt Disnae.

Burning a Rowan Twig

One of Scotland's oldest winter traditions is the burning of a rowan twig. This practice is thought to clear any bad feelings between family and friends – so make sure that you have one handy at the Christmas dinner table!

Rowan trees hold special significance in Scottish culture. They were worshipped by Celtic Druids and planted by doorways to ward off witches. The red colour of the rowan berries was considered to be the most powerful colour for fending off evil, and the five-pointed star on the base of the berries resembles the protective symbol of the pentagram. Rowan trees feature frequently in Scottish folklore and fairy tales, and are often found next to standing stones. They have many Scots names including: quicken, raun, rodden, rone berry, rone tree, roddintree and rountree.

Winter-time

Late lies the wintry sun a-bed,
A frosty, fiery sleepy-head;
Blinks but an hour or two; and then,
A blood-red orange, sets again.

Before the stars have left the skies,
At morning in the dark I rise;
And shivering in my nakedness,
By the cold candle, bathe and dress.

Close by the jolly fire I sit
To warm my frozen bones a bit;
Or with a reindeer-sled, explore
The colder countries round the door.

When to go out, my nurse doth wrap
Me in my comforter and cap;
The cold wind burns my face, and blows
Its frosty pepper up my nose.

Black are my steps on silver sod;
Thick blows my frosty breath abroad;
And tree and house, and hill and lake,
Are frosted like a wedding-cake.

Robert Louis Stevenson

Christmas Fact #1

Scotland is home to the UK's only free-ranging reindeer herd.

Wild reindeer used to roam Scotland until they were hunted to extinction in the thirteenth century. They were re-introduced in the Cairngorms in 1952 by a Swedish reindeer herder called Mikel Utsi, who visited the area on his honeymoon. Today there are around 150 reindeer in the herd, which ranges across the Cairngorm Mountains and the Glenlivet Estate. In 2022, the herd welcomed a trio of rare white reindeer calves.

Crom Dubh na Nollaig

There are many stories of kind magical creatures who help to ensure that Christmas is enjoyed by children every year – Santa's elves, the fairy on top of the Christmas tree, and of course Rudolph and the other reindeer. But many Christmas tales in Scotland describe very different festive beings. We have already been introduced to the mischievous trows, and there is also a legend of an evil spirit who terrorises children during the Christmas season.

On the Hebridean island of Islay, children are warned of the *Crom Dubh na Nollaig* – the Dark Crooked One of Christmas. If they are naughty the *Crom Dubh na Nollaig* will come down the chimney and steal their presents. The howling winds blowing down the islanders' chimneys are said to be the evil creature shrieking in rage. Probably a more effective deterrent of bad behaviour than the threat of a bit of coal in your Christmas stocking!

Playing Tricks

An established part of old Scottish Yule celebrations were 12 days of mayhem and mischief, overseen by an official 'Abbot of Unreason'. It is thought that the custom links back to the Roman feast of Saturnalia. The practice was suppressed in the sixteenth century, and the intricacies of the tradition faded over time, but unsurprisingly, mischievous children continued to embrace the opportunity to cause mayhem for centuries.

Often the trickery would start on Christmas Eve, when anything that could be moved was at risk. Children were known to remove wheels from carts, stuff chimneys with turf or cover them with washtubs, block doorways with boxes and even move boats to unusual locations.

The Christmas Tree on the Mound, Edinburgh

Since the days of the Vikings, Scotland and Norway have shared a connection. This relationship was permanently solidified during the Second World War when Norway was occupied by Nazi Germany. Over 7,000 Norwegians fled to Scotland, earning the coastal town of Buckie in Moray the alternative title of 'Little Norway'. Once safely in Scotland, Norwegian resistance fighters formed specialist units and together with the British army they established the 'Shetland Bus', a clandestine fleet of fishing boats which transferred troops and supplies across the North Sea to support resistance fighters still operating in Norway.

When the war finally came to an end the Norwegian city of Vestland gifted the people of Scotland a gigantic Christmas Tree. To this day every Christmas one of these huge trees is installed on the Mound in Edinburgh, where it stands as a symbol of peace and friendship. The trees were originally felled in the forests of Norway and shipped across to Edinburgh. Today they are sourced in Scotland but remain a gift from the people of Norway.

The Thirteen Days of Yule

This carol is the Scots version of 'The Twelve Days of Christmas' and was sung as far back as the 1800s. The author is unknown, but it featured in Robert Chambers' *Popular Rhymes of Scotland* published in 1842. It should be sung to the tune of 'The Twelve Days of Christmas'. Here is the final verse:

> The King sent his lady on the thirteenth
>   Yule day,
> Three stalks o merry corn, three maids
>   a-merry dancing,
> Three hinds a-merry hunting,
>   an Arabian baboon,
> Three swans a-merry swimming,
>   three ducks a-merry laying,
> A bull that was brown,
> Three goldspinks,* three starlings,
>   a goose that was grey,
> Three plovers, three partridges and
>   a papingoe,** aye.
> Who learns my carol and carries it away.

* goldspinks are goldfinches
** a papingoe is a parrot

Yule Bread

According to F. Marian McNeill's *The Scots Kitchen*, Yule bread was 'a thin bannock of oatmeal cut into quarters to symbolise the cross'. Other reports claim that the bread was shaped in a circle to represent the sun. They usually contained caraway seeds as a charm for protection and to encourage love. These cakes were made at daybreak on Christmas morning and each member of the family was given one. Anyone who was able to keep their bannock unbroken until the evening meal would have good luck for the following year. Recipes for the bannocks vary, but most follow the basic steps below.

INGREDIENTS
25g oatmeal
300ml buttermilk
200g plain flour
½ tsp sugar
½ tsp caraway seeds
½ tsp baking soda

METHOD
1. Soak the oatmeal in buttermilk for several days.
2. Drain the oatmeal and add the flour, sugar, caraway seeds and baking soda.
3. Knead into a soft dough, roll out and bake on a griddle (or dry frying pan) until the outside is toasted and the inside is cooked through.

Working

Christmas was banned by the Presbyterian Church in Scotland in the 1500s and became illegal officially in 1640. Anyone who dared to celebrate was fined or publicly humiliated. Not wanting to miss out on a party, Scots turned their festive focus to Hogmanay and it became Scotland's principal winter festival for almost 400 years. Christmas Day was treated much like any other day – children went to school, people went to work and worshippers only attended church if Christmas Day fell on a Sunday.

It wasn't until 1958 that Christmas Day became a public holiday in Scotland, and even then it was usually a very low-key affair. Many people chose to work rather than lose a day of annual leave. There are stories of the postie delivering the mail on Christmas Day (sometimes a little worse for wear having been offered a dram or two along his route), and family travelling by bus to come for Christmas dinner. Farm hands would work as usual, and in fact often did extra work on Christmas Day so that they could take time off over Hogmanay.

Gradually the influence of American and English attitudes to Christmas began to spread, and finally, after much petitioning, both Christmas Day and Boxing Day officially became bank holidays in 1971.

Celebrating Christmas in January

For many thousands of years Scotland followed the 365-day Julian calendar. However, there were slight inaccuracies with this system, resulting in the gradual addition of three days every four centuries. To help bring our calendar dates back in line with the spring equinox, we officially adopted the Gregorian calendar in 1752, along with the rest of the UK, which brought Christmas Day forward by 11 days.

In reality, many Scottish communities were so isolated that they were either unaware of the conversion, or too stubborn to change. In the remote islands of Shetland the Julian calendar survived rather longer than elsewhere. Even today Christmas is celebrated in January on the island of Foula, 15 miles off Shetland. Residents of this remote island continued to celebrate Christmas on 5 January (25 December according to the old system) for nearly half a century, until the year 1800. This was a leap year in the Julian calendar, but crucially *not* in the Gregorian calendar. Foula Christmas Day therefore moved to 6 January, with New Year moving to the 13th, and there they have remained to the present day. The next time the two calendars will have a leap year clash is 2100 – who knows what will happen to the Foula traditions then?

No Christmas Tree

Christmas trees, while popular in England since the 1860s, were almost unheard of in Scotland until the 1950s, but once the tradition took hold, the trees were adopted with enthusiasm and today Scotland has a thriving Christmas tree industry, with over 700,000 home-grown trees sold each year. However, despite their popularity, it hasn't always been possible for Scots to bring real trees into their homes. For those on the islands, where trees are scarce, Christmas trees often have to be shipped over by boat, which sometimes presents some festive challenges. During the 1967 foot-and-mouth outbreak, imports of Christmas trees to Shetland were banned as part of the measures put in place to control the disease, and artificial trees had to be swiftly sourced as replacements.

A GUID NEW YEAR
AN' MONY O' THEM

The First Christmas Card

It has long been accepted that the first commercial Christmas card was produced in London in 1843 by Sir Henry Cole. It wasn't until 1946, when an Edinburgh scrap metal collector unexpectedly discovered two badly corroded printing plates that the story of the first Christmas card was questioned. The two plates were both engraved with the same image of a laughing, chubby-cheeked boy. One of the plates reads 'A Guid New Year, An' Mony O' Them', while the other says, 'Wishing You A Merry Christmas And A Happy New Year'.

The plates were used to print New Year greetings cards by printer and publisher Charles Drummond, and sold from his shop in the Kirkgate in Leith in 1841 – two years prior to Cole's London version. There is unfortunately no reliable record of any cards printed using the Christmas message. However, the existence of the Christmas printing plate, gives good reason to suspect that the idea of the Christmas card originated in Scotland. Indeed, the design of the laughing face surrounded by a festive message was later to become a common motif in Christmas cards, suggesting that Scotland's first Christmas card had wide-ranging influence.

What do you call
a pigeon that goes
to Aviemore for its
Christmas holidays?

*

A *sgian-dubh*.

Irn Bru Christmas Adverts

In 2006 Irn Bru released one of their most popular TV adverts, a pastiche of Raymond Briggs' animated Christmas film, *The Snowman*. The advert features a ginger-haired boy holding a can of Irn Bru while flying over iconic Scottish landmarks like the Forth Rail Bridge and the Falkirk Wheel with his magical snowman. The accompanying music satires the famous original 'Walking in the Air' lyrics, as the boy and the snowman fall out over the fizzy drink.

The advert proved to be so successful that twelve years later a sequel was commissioned, and the two adverts are now a seasonal staple and have been aired every year since their creation. They have generated such national affection that they have been described as Scotland's version of the American Christmas Coca Cola truck advert.

Whipkull

Whipkull (or whipkül) is Shetland's answer to eggnog. The drink is thought to originate in Scandinavia and is traditionally made with cream, eggs, nutmeg and rum. People have also been known to substitute the rum for whisky. It is drunk at the end of a Yule feast and sometimes even as a breakfast drink on New Year's Day.

INGREDIENTS
12 egg yolks
200g caster sugar
8 tbsp rum or whisky
350ml double cream
1 tsp nutmeg

METHOD
1. Whisk together the egg yolks, sugar and rum.
2. Add the cream.
3. Pour the whipkull into glasses and dust with nutmeg.

Christmas Fact #2

Department store Santas were invented by a Scot.

After emigrating to America, Edinburgh-born James Edgar opened a department store in Massachusetts. In December 1890, he dressed up as Santa and walked around his store handing out gifts to visiting children. Word quickly spread and families flocked to the store to see him. Demand was so high that he had to hire a second Santa to share the role. The following year hundreds of stores across America copied his idea, leading to a tradition that continues throughout the world.

The First Selfie Christmas Card

Today families all over the world photograph themselves in matching Christmas pyjamas so that they will have a festive picture to make into a card when Christmas comes. Some plan this several months in advance, temporarily retrieving their Christmas decorations from storage in the middle of summer to create the perfect selfie Christmas card.

The fascination with festive selfies dates all the way back to Scotland in 1891. At that time Annie Oakley, the famous sharp-shooting star of *Buffalo Bill's Wild West Show* was touring Scotland. Wanting to send a Christmas message to her friends and family back home in the States, she went to a Glasgow printer and requested to have a card produced featuring a portrait of herself.

Annie went on to send similar cards for many years, creating a tradition that, judging by the current obsession with selfies, will doubtless continue for centuries to come.

Artificial Christmas Trees

Scots love Christmas trees, even when they're not actually trees at all. The town of Ullapool has become famous for erecting a community tree made entirely of fishing creels. The installation stands at an impressive nine metres tall. There is also a distillery on the small island of Raasay where staff created their own whisky tree made of over 50 whisky casks. Not to be outdone, the Scottish Borders also boast a Christmas tree made of books at Abbotsford, Sir Walter Scott's house, and the South Lanarkshire town of Strathaven have a 'Ninja' tree – the result of yarn bombing by The Strathaven Combat Crochet and Knitting Ninjas, who describe themselves as 'the Banksies of the yarn craft world'. Dundee even has a competition each year for people to design sustainable Christmas trees made of recycled materials. Entries to date have included trees made of aluminium cans, fabric, vinyl records and old pallets.

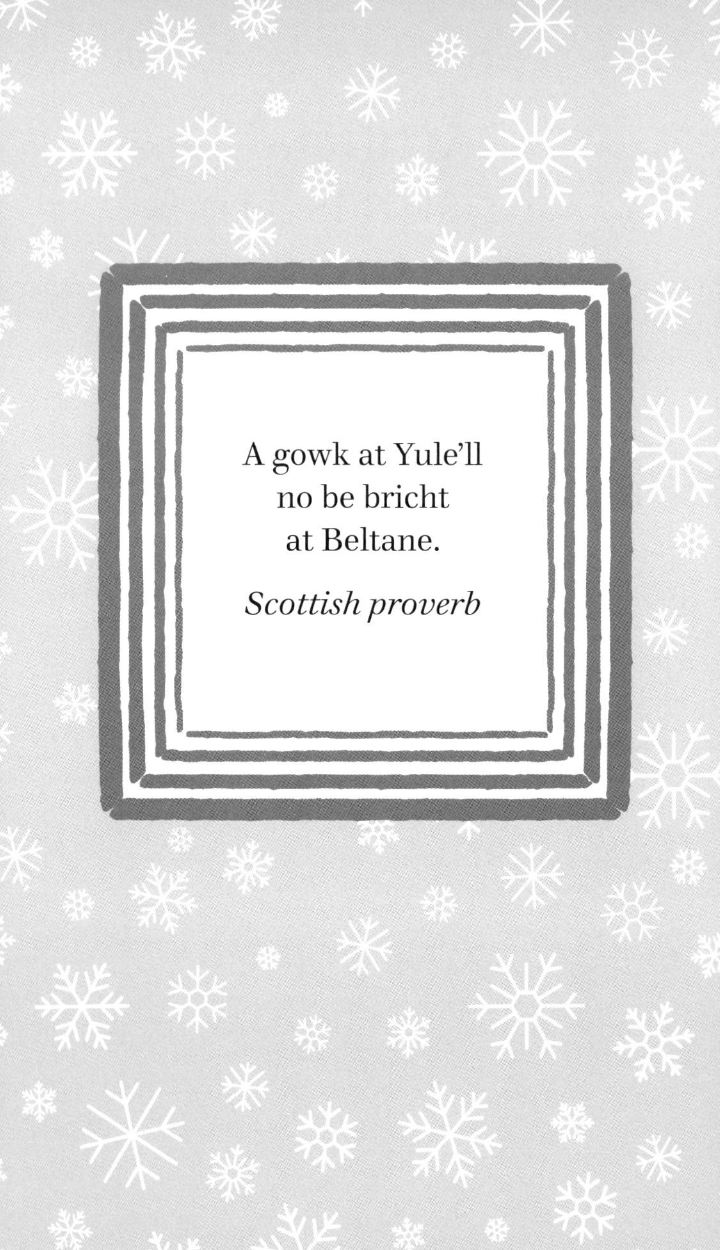
A gowk at Yule'll
no be bricht
at Beltane.

Scottish proverb

The Yule Beggar

This old Scottish Christmas tale is said to originate from the 1500s and links to the belief that St Ninian returns to Galloway every Christmas Eve, only revealing himself to simple shepherds.

One Christmas Eve in Galloway, a young shepherd boy was left in charge of the flock. As evening approached he dutifully gathered all the sheep from the hills and brought them into the pens for the night – all except one ewe. The young shepherd searched and searched for the ewe. The light faded, and he kept searching into the night. Just as he was beginning to lose all hope of finding his precious sheep the boy remembered St Ninian's well, which lay nearby. He had heard that people brought gifts to the well and asked for the saint's help. He also knew that St Ninian was rumoured to return to Galloway every Christmas Eve.

But what could a poor shepherd boy bring as a gift for the great saint? All he possessed were his ragged clothes and a wee bowl of porridge that he was saving for his supper. Ignoring his hunger, the boy carefully carried his bowl of porridge to the well where he prayed to St Ninian to help him find his lost sheep. The boy opened his eyes and looked about him, hoping that his sheep would appear, but there was still no sign of the missing ewe.

Dejected, the young shepherd turned away from the well. Behind him he heard a quiet slurping sound. Turning he saw a thin, ragged man sitting on the side of the well drinking the bowl of porridge.

The beggar waved his spoon at the boy. 'You'll find your sheep caught in a bramble bush in the deep ditch beneath the willow trees that always bloom first in the spring.'

The boy shook his head. 'I've been along that ditch a dozen times, and it's not there.' But the beggar was insistent and led the young shepherd to the place he had described.

To the boy's amazement there was the ewe, caught in thorns deep in the ditch. Together the beggar and the boy worked to free the sheep's knotted wool from the thorns and carried the exhausted animal back to the flock.

The boy invited the beggar to spend the night next to his fire. To his surprise the beggar declined: 'It's a kind offer. But I must be on my way or I'll be late.'

'Late?' exclaimed the boy. 'But where are you going? It's nearly midnight.'

'Bethlehem, of course!' replied the beggar.

And with that the beggar disappeared, leaving only a glittering trail of frost leading to the east. The boy realised that he had been blessed with St Ninian's help and vowed that he would return to the well every Christmas Eve to give thanks to the saint.

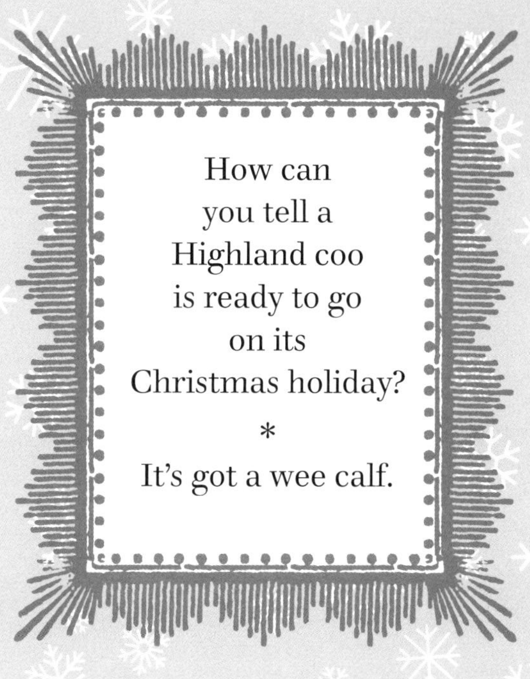
How can
you tell a
Highland coo
is ready to go
on its
Christmas holiday?
*
It's got a wee calf.

Christmas Fact #3

Robert Louis Stevenson gave away his birthday as a Christmas gift.

Upon hearing that a friend's daughter was upset at having a Christmas birthday, Robert Louis Stevenson drafted a mock legal document transferring his birthday on 13 November to the little girl. He claimed to have reached an age where 'I have no further use for a birthday', and trusted her to make better use of the day than he could. He would have been around 42 at the time.

Fortune Telling

Scotland has a rich heritage of fortune telling, from reading meaning in the shapes of ashes in a fire to understanding the significance of marks on mutton bones. On Christmas Eve some families would gather together, and each unmarried member would crack an egg in a glass. The shape of the egg white was said to indicate the occupation of their future spouse. The eggs were then used with oatmeal and milk to make individual bannocks. Each bannock was marked by a member of the household. If the bannock broke during cooking it was thought to be bad luck.

Bannocks were also made for Yule celebrations, sometimes containing good luck tokens. Whoever found the trinket would have good luck for the following year.

The Broons and Oor Wullie Annuals

Many Scots will remember tearing the wrapping from a Broons or Oor Wullie annual on Christmas morning. These annuals, collating a year's worth of Dudley Watkins' and Ken Harrison's famous comic strips from *The Sunday Post* newspaper, have been a staple Christmas present in Scotland for over 80 years.

Since 1939 The Broons and Oor Wullie annuals have been published on alternating years, interrupted only by Second World War paper shortages. When the annuals were first published they were usually sold by newsagents rather than bookshops, and were considered to be disposable (like the newspapers in which they first appeared), and so were not collected by libraries. Many of the early editions are therefore extremely scarce and are now valuable collectors' items fetching several thousand pounds on the rare occasions that they come up for auction. Even the National Library of Scotland, which aims to hold copies of every book ever published in Scotland, had to search for over a decade to find a copy of the first ever Broons annual.

They eventually completed their collection of annuals just in time for Christmas 2023.

How I'll Decorate My Tree

It was still very far from Christmas
when my mamma said to me:
tell me, Precious, what *you* going to hang
on *our* Christmas tree?

I said: the fairy-lights that Dad just fixed
and . . . jewel-coloured jelly-beans from the
    pick'n'mix –
oh, and from it I'll dangle tinsel in tangles,
sparkles, sequins and spangles,
a round golden coin (chocolate money),
that cracker joke that was *actually funny*,
my rosary beads – and a plastic rose
as red as Rudolph Reindeer's nose,
the gnome that grows the tangerines,
the picture of me with my tambourine,
and (this is Mum's favourite, she says)
the photo of all of us in our PJ's!
The Ladybird book that Lola lent me,
the blue butterfly bracelet that Brittany sent me,
the ear-ring I lost,
a pop-up Jack Frost,
a space-hopper, an everlasting gobstopper,
a pink-eyed sugar mouse,
the keys to my grandfather's house,
a tiny pair of trainers with silver laces,
and – now my smile is straight – gonna hang up my
    braces!

A marble, an angel-scrap, a star,
the very last sweetie out my advent calendar,
a kiss under the mistletoe,
a mitten still cracked with a crunch and a creak of
   snow,
that glitter scarf I finally got sick of,
a spoon with cake-mix still to lick off,
the Dove of Peace that our Darren made,
some green thoughts in our tree's green shade –
I'll hang up every evergreen memory
of moments as melted and gone
as that candle that was *supposed* to smell
of cinnamon –
memories big as a house and as small's
the baubles I used to call *ball-balls.*

With pleasure I'll treasure them
then, on *proper* Christmas Day, I'll show them all to
   you
between the Queen's Speech and *Doctor Who.*

Liz Lochhead

Yule Log

This rich and creamy Yule log is not for the faint-hearted – it's a decadent triple-chocolate Christmas treat, but it's as easy as making a Swiss roll.

Preparation time: over 2 hours
Cooking time: 30 mins to 1 hour
Serves 8

INGREDIENTS
vegetable oil, for greasing
150g golden caster sugar
6 large free-range eggs, separated
250g high quality dark chocolate
    (minimum 60 per cent cocoa solids)

For the buttercream icing filling:
250g unsalted butter, softened
450g golden icing sugar, plus extra for dusting
50g cocoa powder, sifted
2 tbsp milk

For the cream filling:
400ml double cream, lightly whipped
250g raspberries
dash whisky liqueur (optional)

METHOD

1. This Christmas roll can be made two ways: with buttercream icing and festive decorations, or filled with cream and berries.
2. Preheat the oven to 220°C/425°F/Gas 7. Line a 23 × 33cm Swiss roll tin with greaseproof paper and brush this lightly with oil.
3. Combine the caster sugar and egg yolks in a bowl and whisk them together until light and thick. Melt the chocolate with 4 tbsp cold water in a bowl over a pan of very gently simmering water. When you can see the chocolate has melted until smooth, stir in the sugar and egg mixture.
4. Meanwhile, whisk the egg whites until stiff but not dry. Gently fold a spoonful of the egg whites into the chocolate mixture to lighten it, then fold in the remaining whites using a large metal spoon. Do not overmix, and always use a gentle action. Pour the batter gently into the prepared tin and bake for 12–14 minutes (no longer), until risen and just firm to the touch.
5. Remove to a wire rack and leave to cool in the tin for at least 2 hours.
6. Once cold, lay a sheet of greaseproof paper on a board. With one bold movement, turn the whole cake onto the sheet of paper, then lift the tin off. Carefully peel away the paper and trim away any scraggy edges of cake.

7. To make the buttercream icing, beat the butter until soft, then sift in the icing sugar and cocoa. Add the milk and combine together until soft. Spread half the icing over the cake up to the edges.
8. Roll up as you would a Swiss roll: starting at the long side opposite you, use the paper to roll the cake towards you, around the icing; don't worry about the cracks. Transfer to a flat serving dish. Carefully spread the remaining icing over the cake (you can pipe the icing if you like). Chill until needed, then decorate with festive decorations and sift over some icing sugar.
9. To make the cream filling, spread the inverted cake with the whipped cream, scatter over the berries and add a few dribbles of Drambuie, if you like. Carefully roll up as described above. Sift over icing sugar just before serving.

Christmas Fact #4

Sir Alex Ferguson once launched a range of Christmas trees.

In 2015, Sir Alex Ferguson was asked to put his name to an artificial Christmas tree by a friend and neighbour who owned Christmas Tree World in Wigan. The 12-foot artificial 'Ferguson Fir', was pre-fitted with white or coloured LED lights and cost £69.99. They also sold an 'Ultra Ferguson' tree with additional branch tips, more lights and a range of different settings, priced at £83.99.

Child in the Manger

Over 150 years ago a crofter named Mary Macdonald created what was to become one of the world's most beautiful carols and a chart-topping pop song. Mary's original lyrics were later rewritten as 'Morning Has Broken' and became famous the world over when the song was recorded by Yusuf /Cat Stevens in 1971. It went on to reach Number 9 in the UK charts.

Below are the original Gaelic lyrics with their English translation.

Leanabh an àigh, an Leanabh aig Màiri
Rugadh san stàball, Rìgh nan Dùl;
Thàinig do'n fhàsach, dh'fhuiling 'n ar n-àite
Son' iad an àireamh bhitheas dhà dlùth!

Ged a bhios leanabain aig rìghrean na talmhainn
An greadhnachas garbh is anabarr mùirn,
'S geàrr gus am falbh iad, 's fasaidh iad anfhann,
An àilleachd 's an dealbh a' searg san ùir.

Cha b'ionann 's an t-Uan thàinig gur fuasgladh
Iriosal, stuama ghluais e'n tùs;
E naomh gun truailleachd, Cruithfhear an t-sluaigh,
Dh'éirich e suas le buaidh o ùir.

Child in the manger, infant of Mary,
Outcast and stranger, Lord of all,
Child who inherits all our transgressions,
All our demerits on Him fall.

Once the most holy Child of salvation
Gently and lowly lived below;
Now as our glorious mighty Redeemer,
See Him victorious o'er each foe.

Prophets foretold Him, infant of wonder;
Angels behold Him on His throne;
Worthy our Savior of all our praises;
Happy forever are His own.

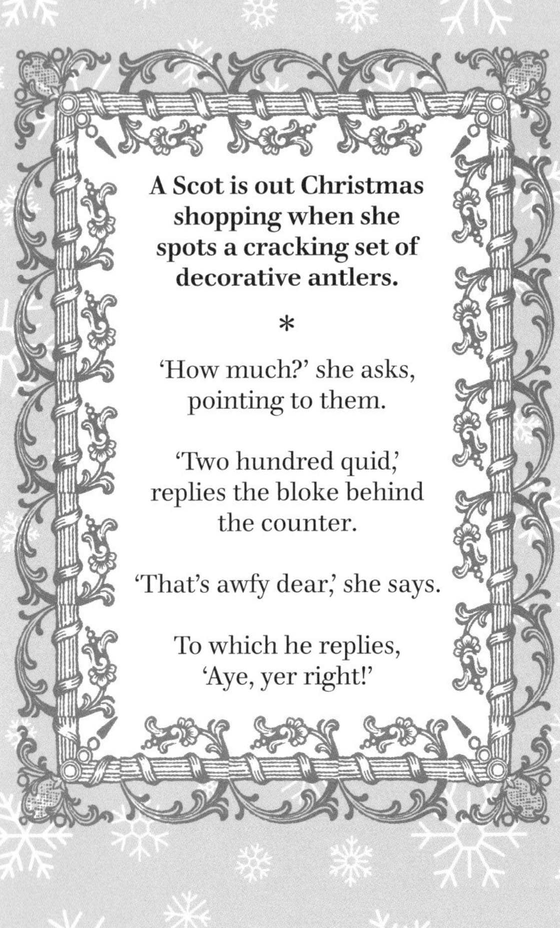

A Scot is out Christmas
shopping when she
spots a cracking set of
decorative antlers.

*

'How much?' she asks,
pointing to them.

'Two hundred quid,'
replies the bloke behind
the counter.

'That's awfy dear,' she says.

To which he replies,
'Aye, yer right!'

Football

The tradition of kicking a ball about on Christmas Day or New Year's Day dates back many hundreds of years. There is a particularly strong heritage in the north of Scotland. The oldest known reference was made on 25 December 1600 and describes a game of 'futball' played in the Chanonrie Kirk in Elgin.

These Christmas matches were extremely popular but could also be unbelievably violent. There is a laboriously long but delightfully gruesome eighteenth-century poem called 'The Monymusk Christmas Ba'ing', which describes how some Monymusk villagers 'yowff'd the ba' frae dyke to dkye', and 'clash'd Geordie's scull/ Hard to the steeple wa''. The last verse sums up the account of the extensive injuries sustained during the match:

> Has ne'er in Monymuss been seen
> Sae mony weel-beft skins:
> Of a' the bawmen there was nane
> But had twa bleedy shins.

A White Christmas

Who doesn't dream of a white Christmas? In the eighteenth and nineteenth centuries this was a relatively common occurrence in Scotland, and even more so before the change to the Gregorian calendar in 1752 that effectively brought Christmas Day forward by 11 days.

The Met Office declares a white Christmas when a single snowflake is observed falling on Christmas Day. While widespread Christmas snow cover is rare and has only occurred a handful of times in living memory, over half of Scotland's Christmases have officially been white since 1960. The snowiest year on record was 1995, when 77 different locations in Scotland recorded snowfall. But the continuing tradition of our white Christmases is uncertain. Over the past decade the number of December days with snow on the ground has dwindled, the North of Scotland in particular has seen a 30 per cent reduction in snow days. Meanwhile, in Exeter on Christmas Day in 2023 there were temperatures of over 13°C. Perhaps in the future we will have to be content to dream of a dry Christmas rather than a white one …

Christmas Fact #5

The King's Christmas Day speech was inspired by a Scot.

In 1932, Stonehaven-born Sir John Reith, Director General of the BBC, suggested that King George V record a Christmas message for radio from a small office in Sandringham Palace. The King had previously refused to make a recording when asked in 1922, but Sir John Reith eventually managed to persuade him to take part and the resulting transmission proved so popular that it immediately become a steadfast part of Christmas Day.

Cock-A-Leekie Soup

Cock-a-leekie was originally a type of stew known as potage and would have been regular winter food for those not sufficiently well-off to indulge in great Christmas feasts. Potage is an old word for meals cooked in a pot with whatever came to hand. The resulting stew could be added to whenever fresh ingredients were available and often lasted for days or even weeks.

INGREDIENTS
4 leeks
1 small whole chicken (giblets removed)
4 carrots, roughly chopped
2 sticks of celery, roughly chopped
2 bay leaves
2 litres cold water
120g long grain rice
salt and pepper to taste
handful of prunes (optional)

METHOD
1. Remove the green parts of the leeks and place in the bottom of a large soup pot. Place the chicken on top and surround with 2 carrots, the celery and bay leaves.
2. Add enough cold water to cover the chicken (approx. 2 litres).
3. Bring to the boil then simmer for 1 hour, until the chicken's juices run clear.

4. Remove the chicken and pour the stock through a colander into a bowl (not down the sink!), then pour it back into the soup pot.
5. Add the chopped whites of the leeks and the 2 remaining carrots. Cook for 10 minutes.
6. Add the rice and simmer for 15 minutes until cooked.
7. Shred the chicken, removing all bones, and add it to the broth.
8. Allow the chicken to heat through for a few minutes. Season to taste.
9. Serve sprinkled with slices of prune.

Christmas Fact #6

In 2011 an Ayrshire man was admitted to the Golden Jubilee Hospital in Clydebank for eating too many Brussels sprouts.

The high levels of vitamin K in the Christmas dinner vegetable counteracted the anticoagulants that the man was taking. The case was reported in a festive edition of the Medical Journal of Australia, and the hospital are reported as saying, 'We think this is possibly the first-ever festive admission to hospital caused by the consumption of Brussels sprouts.' After diagnosis the man was quickly stabilised.

Words for Snow

It is a myth that Eskimos have more than 50 words for snow, but it is true that Scots have over 400. The Historical Thesaurus of Scots project at the University of Glasgow has found hundreds of different terms relating to snow in their research cataloguing Scots vocabulary (though surprisingly there are only around 100 words relating to rain). Here is a wee selection:

Blin-drift: Drifting snow
Feefle: Swirling snow
Feuchter: Lightly falling snow
Flindrikin: A light snow shower
Flukra: Snow falling in large flakes
Owerblaw: To be covered with snow
Skalva: Soft, flaky snow
Skelf: A large snowflake
Skiff: Very light snowfall
Skovin: A large snowflake
Smirr: Fine sleet or snow
Snaw: Snow
Snaw-pouther: Fine, driving snow
Sneesl: To begin to snow
Spitters: Small flakes of wind-driven snow
Unbrak: Snow beginning to thaw
Yird drift: Snow blown from the ground

The Kirkwall Ba' Game

The Kirkwall Ba' Game is perhaps Scotland's most notorious Christmas football tradition. This chaotic battle takes place on the streets (and reportedly even the rooftops) of Kirkwall in Orkney. The game is fought between two rival Orcadian factions, the Uppies and the Doonies, each striving to secure a goal with a handmade leather-and-cork ball.

The earliest known records of the game are 300 years old, but originally it is thought to stem from the ancient celebrations of the winter solstice. There is a grizzly legend that claims that the game commemorates the defeat of a tyrant named Tusker who was hunted down and beheaded by a young Orcadian man. While riding home with Tusker's severed head on his saddle, the young man is scratched by one of Tusker's teeth. The wound becomes infected, and the dying boy staggers through the streets of Kirkwall, finally throwing the head into the gathered crowd as he collapses. Enraged at Tusker for this final posthumous act of vindictiveness, the townsfolk kick his head through the Kirkwall streets, and so the ba' game was born.

On his way home from a
boozy Christmas party a
Glaswegian man sees his
neighbour tinkering with
the engine of his car.

*

He asks him, 'What's up?'
The neighbour replies,
'Piston broke.'
Man says, 'Aye, me too.'

O Come All Ye Faithful

Scholars have recently proposed that the Christmas carol, 'O Come All Ye Faithful', was not written as a celebration of the birth of Christ, but was in fact a coded Jacobite call to arms, sung to honour the birth of Bonnie Prince Charlie.

The earliest known copy is devoted to '*regem nostrum Jacobum*', namely James III, Bonnie Prince Charlie's father. Copies are often illustrated with Jacobite floral imagery, such as the white rose, and the original Latin lyrics are thought to contain a pun on *Angelorum* (angels) and *Anglorum* (English). So, the line 'Come and Behold Him, Born the King of Angels' may actually mean, 'Come and Behold Him, Born the King of the English'. By the time the hymn was translated into English the Jacobite cause had waned and the coded messages had been forgotten.

Sweetie Scone Day

Today, Boxing Day is often associated with shopping, but traditionally it was dedicated to the giving of alms or donations to the needy. In some parts of Scotland the day was affectionately known as Sweetie Scone Day. The name derives from the time when Scotland's lairds had vast numbers of servants and estate workers. On 26 December the laird and his lady would gather their workers together and give gifts of 'sweetieskons' – fruit cakes laden with sultanas, currants and spices. In some cases there are reports that the laird provided the expensive ingredients and the remainder were supplemented by other members of the community, who would also bake the cakes and distribute them among the poorer households.

Christmas Fact #7

On Boxing Day 1900 it was discovered that three lighthouse keepers had mysteriously disappeared from the Flannan Isles Lighthouse.

On 26 December 1900 a routine visit of relief staff to the Flannan Isles Lighthouse in the Outer Hebrides could find no sign of the three lighthouse keepers who had been stationed there over Christmas. An untouched meal was set out on the table, the lamps were trimmed and ready, and the lens and machinery cleaned – but there was no trace of the missing men. To this day their disappearance remains a mystery. Theories about their fate have included murder, ghosts and alien abduction. But the most commonly accepted idea is that the unlucky keepers were simply washed away by a wave.

Cloutie Dumpling

Scotland's answer to the Christmas pudding, cloutie (or clootie) dumping is a celebratory boiled pudding often eaten at Christmas and Hogmanay.

Serves 6–8

INGREDIENTS

2–3 tbsp flour
125g beef suet, finely chopped, or Atora pre-prepared
100g self-raising flour
175g fine white breadcrumbs
25g fine oatmeal
1 tsp baking powder
350g raisins/sultanas mixed
2-3 tsp each of ground cinnamon, ginger and
    mixed spice
1 large tart cooking apple, peeled and grated
1 large carrot, grated
2 tbsp black treacle
2 tbsp golden syrup
2 tbsp Seville orange marmalade
2 eggs
Fresh orange juice to mix

You will also need:
55cm/22in diameter close-textured, strong white cotton or linen cloth; length of string; large pot with lid, small saucer.

METHOD

1. Half-fill a very large pot with water and bring to the boil. Place an upside-down saucer in the base to prevent the dumpling sticking. Add the cloth to the boiling water and boil for a few minutes.
2. Lift the cloth out and allow excess water to drip off then lay flat on a table. Dust a thick layer of flour over the whole cloth while still hot. Shake off the excess.
3. Put suet, flour, breadcrumbs, oatmeal, baking powder, sultanas, raisins and spices into a large mixing bowl. Add the apple and carrot.
4. Put the syrup, treacle, marmalade and eggs into a small bowl and mix together with a fork till the syrup and treacle are dissolved.
5. Add the syrup mix to the dry ingredients and combine. There should be enough moisture to make a soft but not sloppy consistency. Add orange juice if it is very stiff.
6. Put the mixture into the centre of the prepared cloth. Draw up the edges, leaving some room for the dumpling to expand, and tie tightly with string, leaving an extra length of string to tie onto the pot handles. Pat the dumpling into a round shape.
7. Add the dumpling to the pot. The water should come about half way up. Tie the string to the handles so that the dumpling is held in position.
8. Cover and simmer gently for about 4 hours. Check the water-level regularly.
9. Fill a large basin or sink with cold water. Holding the dumpling by the string, dip it into cold water for about 60 seconds.
10. Open the cloth and carefully remove the dumpling.
11. Dry off in the oven or in front of the fire until the skin forms, becoming a burnished, brown colour.

Rugby

For Scotland's rugby fans, the festive season offers some excellent opportunities to enjoy a game. For more than 150 years Edinburgh and Glasgow have sought to settle their long-standing rivalry and brighten the lull between Christmas and Hogmanay with two highly popular rugby union fixtures. These games are known as the 1872 Cup and are the oldest inter-district rugby contest in the world, pre-dating the creation of Scottish Rugby Union by four months. The contest has a complicated history but now takes the form of a derby between Glasgow and Edinburgh's professional sides, Glasgow Warriors and Edinburgh Rugby.

Perhaps the most bizarre part of the history of this derby is that from the outset there was no trophy, or tangible award of any kind. It wasn't until 1995, over 120 years after the competition began, when sponsors came on board to fund a genuine cup, that the game finally got a prize.

Robbie Anderson and the Trows

*This is a traditional Hogmanay
folk tale from Shetland.*

Robbie Anderson lived on the Shetland island of Yell with his wife and children. They did not have much money, but they were happy fishing and tending their croft. Robbie was known as the best fiddle player on the island.

One Christmas Eve Robbie was checking his sheep when he came across a wee man with red hair. He knew instantly that this wee man was a trow, one of Shetland's fairy folk. The trow told Robbie that he was to come and play at the trows' Hogmanay party. Robbie, knowing trows to be mischievous creatures, tried to decline, explaining that he usually played for his friends on New Year's Eve.

'If you play for us we will reward you,' said the trow, 'but you must never tell anyone where you have been.'

Robbie was intrigued by the suggestion of a reward, and he knew that trows could be good as well as wicked, so when night fell he tucked his fiddle under his arm and headed off to the place where the trows were known to live.

When Robbie found the trows' party it was already in full swing, and he played for them until the sun rose. Suddenly the party was over and he found himself alone. There had been no reward from the trows, not even a word of thanks. Dejected, Robbie walked home empty handed.

By the end of January the islanders' winter food stores were starting to run low. Robbie and his friends decided to go fishing to help feed their families. Although they were all experienced fishermen none of the islanders caught anything, except for Robbie. He pulled in line after line of wriggling, silver fish. The fish were so easy to catch that he didn't even need to bait his hooks. By the end of the day Robbie had caught enough fish to share among all the islanders.

As spring approached, the islanders gathered their sheep. All of Robbie's friends had lost sheep in the winter storms but Robbie's sheep were all alive and well.

At harvest time the autumn winds blew hard across

the island. The crops of many islanders were destroyed, but Robbie's wheat stood tall and ripe in his fields.

Robbie started to wonder if his good luck through the year was due to the trows. When Hogmanay came round again he made sure that he was in the same place where the trow had found him the year before. Again the trow appeared, and again Robbie agreed to play for the trows' party. Year after year Robbie played, and year after year he had good luck.

Many years later Robbie waited to meet the trow on Hogmanay, but the trow did not come. Confused Robbie went to the trow's house but found no one there except a tiny old trow woman. The old trow told Robbie that all the other trows had fled to the Faroe Islands to avoid the hatred of a new preacher. From that day forward Robbie had no more trowie luck, and his life returned to normal.

Redding the House

Many Scots still follow the tradition of redding (or readying) the house before the New Year. It is believed that you should give your house a thorough cleaning before the New Year starts – or else risk it being a mess for the whole of the year ahead. Some people also believe that they must clear all their debts and settle all their bills before the bells, and the more superstitious will also banish evil spirits by bringing a burning juniper branch into each room of the house.

While doing the high dusting may be part of the redding preparations for some, traditionally the most important piece of housework was clearing the fire. Last thing on New Year's Eve any unburnt coals were removed and the remaining ash spread as smooth as possible. On New Year's morning families would gather to read the ashes, much like reading tea leaves, and make predictions about the coming year. A foot shape with the toes pointing towards the door was believed to signal death, and a foot pointing into the room was said to herald new life. The first fire of the New Year was also carefully monitored. If a coal or peat rolled away from the fire it was believed to be a sign that one of the family would depart in the coming year.

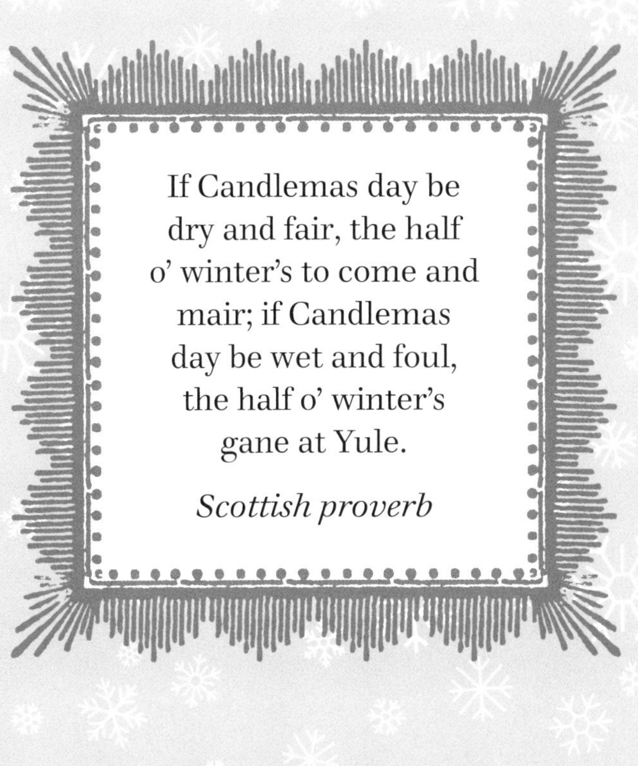

If Candlemas day be
dry and fair, the half
o' winter's to come and
mair; if Candlemas
day be wet and foul,
the half o' winter's
gane at Yule.

Scottish proverb

Hogmanay

Hogmanay is the Scots term for New Year's Eve. The banning of Christmas celebrations in 1640 had a huge influence on the growth and popularity of Hogmanay in Scotland, which became the focus of winter festivities for Scottish people.

The exact origins of Hogmanay have been debated for centuries. The festival itself is thought to have emerged from the combined legacies of the Roman feast of Saturnalia, and the Norse festival of Yule. The origins of the name, pronounced *hog-muh-nay*, are equally uncertain. It may have come from the French word *hoginane*, meaning gala day, or from the Anglo-Saxon *haleg monath*, meaning holy month, or indeed from *hoggo-nott*, the Scandanavian reference to Yule. There is also potential etymology from the Normandy tradition of giving New Year presents called *hoguignetes*. Whatever its roots, for the Scottish people Hogmanay is synonymous with warm hospitality, whisky and energetic celebrations such as ceilidhs and live music.

Winter

Winter doesn't make us better, then, or worse
But enables us to find ourselves again,
Because it forces us to be quiet, obliges us
To listen to the coursing of our own blood;
Winter reminds us that warmth
Is not something that we find naturally,
Some gift of munificent nature, but must be made;
That we should make in Scotland
A small place of warmth, a small country
Of kindness to others, of brotherhood,
Is what our poets have been striving to say
Since they first gave voice to song.
That we might find this, in winter,
In a troubled world, is a local miracle,
To warm the heart, to warm the heart.

Alexander McCall Smith

Hogmanay Santa Claus

The history of Santa Claus is complicated; he appears in differing versions in countries across the world. Scotland is no exception, having their own interpretation of the jolly old elf and his antics. In fact, under his formal title of St Nicholas he is the patron saint of Aberdeen due to his reputation for being a friend and protector of sailors.

It appears that the Scots were early and enthusiastic adopters of the legend of Santa. The first mention of Santa in the British Library's newspaper archive comes from an article in the *John O'Groat Journal* in 1852, where some children in Wick describe hanging their stockings by the fireplace. Apparently, Santa was particularly good to the children of Wick that year gifting buns, toys and books – though one unfortunate child claimed to have received a stick.

Today it is common practice for Scottish children to hang their stockings on Christmas Eve, often leaving Santa a mince pie and a dram of whisky. However, the nineteenth-century children of Wick, and many generations after them, hung their stockings on Hogmanay and opened their presents on New Year's Day. It wasn't until the 1950s that Santa eventually changed his schedule to Christmas Eve.

Petticoat Tails Shortbread

The origin of the name of these dainty shortbread biscuits is likely simply to do with the shape of the biscuits: the wedges are identical in shape to the individual gores of the full, bell-hooped petticoats worn by the ladies at Court – certainly at the time of Mary, Queen of Scots in the sixteenth century, who was said to be fond of them.

Makes 16 triangles

INGREDIENTS

175g butter, softened
75g golden caster sugar + extra to sprinkle on top
175g plain flour
pinch of salt
75g fine semolina or rice flour (or cornflour)

METHOD

1. Butter two 17cm sandwich tins (or one 25cm tin). Preheat the oven to 150°C/300°F/Gas 2.
2. Cream the butter and sugar together until pale; this will take 4–5 minutes in a food mixer or longer by hand.

3. Now add the flour, a good pinch of salt and the semolina/rice flour (or cornflour), a tablespoonful at a time, only adding more when each is incorporated. When it is all mixed in, bring together with your hands and form into one large or two medium balls.
4. Roll out each ball (either by pressing with your palms if you have cold hands or with a very light touch of a rolling pin if your hands are hot) to a circle just a little shy of the size of your prepared tins, then pop into the tin.
5. Prick all over with a fork (ensure you go right through to the base) and 'scallop' the edges by nicking round the edges with the edge of a spoon.
6. If you have time, chill the tins for about 10 minutes, as the dough will be slightly warm, depending how hot your hands are.
7. Place in the oven for 35–40 minutes for the small tins and 40–50 minutes for the large tin, until the biscuits are a pale golden brown.
8. Remove the tins to a wire rack, cut each of the small circles into 8 triangles, and the large circle into 16, and sprinkle over some sugar.
9. Leave for 15–20 minutes or so, then remove from the tin while still a little warm but firm enough to be removed. Leave on a wire rack until cold.

What is the
best Christmas
present in the
world?

*

A broken drum.
Ye cannae beat it!

Burning the Cailleach

The Cailleach is one of Scotland's most ancient mythological figures. She is the Goddess of Winter and a symbol of death, a wizened old crone dressed in grey with a white shawl. As she ushers in the dark days of winter she washes her shawl in the Corryvreckan whirlpools, off the island of Jura. Once the shawl is clean and white the Cailleach lays it upon the hills to dry, covering Scotland in a blanket of snow. Throughout winter she walks through the mountains and valleys, crushing any signs of growth or new life.

On Christmas Eve or Hogmanay, Scots who wanted to banish the cold, hard days of winter would carve or chalk the face of an old woman into a log and burn it upon the fire. This log was known as the *Cailleach Nollich*. As it burned, the face of the old woman would become charred and disappear, and as the log reduced to ashes it was believed that the dark winter days would begin to lengthen, and that death would bypass the household for the following year.

Guising

Guising is Scotland's precursor to 'Trick or Treating' and is usually associated with Halloween (as pictured opposite). However, the tradition of dressing up in ghoulish costumes and parading round the houses is also connected to the celebration of Old Christmas (6 January according to the Julian Calendar) and Hogmanay.

Across many parts of Scotland large groups of men and women, often as many as 20–30 people, would dress up in masks and homemade costumes, with beards made of sheepskins. The men dressed as women and the women as men. They would walk miles from house to house performing skits and songs. Different communities had different customs, and over the centuries children tended to do more of the guising than adults. The islanders of Berneray, off North Uist, still uphold this custom. Each year the children there dress up on Old New Year (12 January) and visit every one of the 60 houses on the island. Any householder who does not allow entry or reward the guisers risks a curse on their house.

Rise Up
Guid Wife

This is a traditional Hogmanay guising song.

Rise up guid wife and shak yer feathers,
Dinna think that we are beggars,
We're wee bairnies come to play,
Rise up and gie's wur Hogmanay.
Hogmanay's a bawbee, a bawbee, a bawbee,
Hogmanay's a bawbee to greet the New Year.

The Stomness Log Pull

Yule logs are another of Scotland's ancient winter customs, stemming back to a time when it was believed that the sun stood still for 12 days in the middle of winter. The Yule log would be lit from the remains of previous year's Yule log and would be kept burning for 12 days to banish evil spirits and bring luck for the coming year.

The people of Stromness in Orkney have a unique Yule log tradition. Attaching ropes or chains to a giant half-ton log in the centre of the town, they hold a tug-of-war, pitting the Northern residents (the North-enders) against those from the South (the Soothenders). The town's two piers serve as goals, and in a battle of strength the contestants drag the log back and forth through the streets until one of the goals is reached and a winner is declared.

The tree used to make the log was traditionally stolen from a local garden on Christmas Eve, but this practice was banned in the 1930s due to the rarity of trees on the island. The Log Pull itself died out entirely for 80 years but was revived in 2017 and now takes place on Hogmanay. The log is no longer stolen but is supplied by a sawmill.

Stonehaven Fireballs

The people of Stonehaven in Aberdeenshire have a uniquely dangerous way to see out the old year and welcome the new. Every Hogmanay they take to the streets, minutes before midnight, swinging blazing balls of fire around their heads as a way to ward off evil spirits.

The balls are wire cages which can often be as big as 50cm in diameter. Each fireballer has their own 'recipe', with everyone striving to keep their ball alight for the duration of the procession.

During the war years the celebrations were stopped as it was feared that the lights would attract enemy bombers, but ever since then the festivities have grown in popularity. The population of Stonehaven now doubles on Hogmanay with visitors coming from far and wide to witness the spectacle. You can even watch the celebrations from anywhere in the world as they are live streamed on the community website.

Deck the Halls

One of the world's favourite Christmas carols, 'Deck the Halls', has been recorded by everyone from Nat King Cole to the Lumineers, and has been used to advertise everything from deodorant to Weetabix. But it actually isn't a song about Christmas at all – it is a carol about Hogmanay.

'Deck the Halls' was originally a sixteenth-century Welsh song named *'Nos Galan'*, but was given English lyrics by the Scottish musician Thomas Oliphant in 1862. Oliphant's lyrics initially included lots of references to drinking – not surprising for a Scottish song about Hogmanay. These were swiftly replaced with more wholesome references to gaiety. Oliphant's original lyrics are given below.

Deck the hall with boughs of holly,
Fa, la, la, la, la, la, la, la, la!
'Tis the season to be jolly:
Fa, la, la, la, la, la, la, la, la!
Fill the meadcup, drain the barrel,
Fa, la, la, la, la, la, la, la, la!
Troul the ancient Christmas carol.
Fa, la, la, la, la, la, la, la, la!

Deck the hall with boughs of holl - y, Fa, la, la, la, la, la,

la, la, la! 'Tis the sea - son to be joll - y:

Fa, la, la, la, la, la, la, la, la! Fill the mead cup,

drain the bar-rel, Fa,la,la, la,la la, la, la, la! Troul the an-cient

Christ-mas ca - rol Fa, la, la, la, la la, la, la, la!

See the flowing bowl before us,
Fa, la, la, la, la, la, la, la!
Strike the harp, and join in chorus:
Fa, la, la, la, la, la, la, la!
Follow me in merry measure,
Fa, la, la, la, la, la, la, la!
While I sing of beauty's treasure.
Fa, la, la, la, la, la, la, la!

Fast away the old year passes,
Fa, la, la, la, la, la, la, la!
Hail the new, ye lads and lasses:
Fa, la, la, la, la, la, la, la!
Laughing quaffing all together,
Fa, la, la, la, la, la, la, la!
Heedless of the wind and weather.
Fa, la, la, la, la, la, la, la!

The Biggar Bonfire

Each Hogmanay the Lanarkshire town of Biggar lights a gigantic bonfire, right in the centre of the high street. The windows of nearby buildings are boarded up to prevent them from cracking in the heat and crowds come from miles around to witness the towering flames.

The celebrations start with a torchlit procession along the high street, accompanied by a pipe band. Biggar's oldest resident then lights the bonfire as onlookers toast the New Year.

It seems that the people of Biggar will stop at almost nothing to keep their tradition alive. Even during the Second World War, when blackout restrictions prevented a full bonfire, a candle in a tin can was placed on the bonfire site. And more recently, when the Covid pandemic and concerns over the proximity of a gas supply pipe put the future of the event in jeopardy, the community fought to retain it. The festival was cancelled for three years but finally returned in 2023. Hopefully it will now continue as a part of our Scottish Hogmanay heritage for many years to come.

Now's now,
and Yule's
in winter.

Scottish proverb

The Comrie Flambeaux

Set in the heart of Scotland, the village of Comrie in Perthshire is home to one of Scotland's many unique Hogmanay fire festivals. Here, as the church bells toll midnight, ten giant torches (the flambeaux) are paraded through the village by a pipe band, with hosts of villagers in fancy dress in their wake. At the end of the parade the torches are cast over the Dalginross Bridge into the waters of the River Earn, symbolising the casting out of evil spirits.

The flambeaux are made from birch saplings wrapped in hessian bags, usually old tattie sacks. They are made on the first Sunday after Armistice Sunday, and are soaked in a drum of paraffin for six weeks before they are ready to use on Hogmanay.

Black Bun

Black bun was supposedly the original Twelfth Night cake eaten in Scotland, before it became known as 'Scotch Christmas Bun' during the first half of the nineteenth century. It was traditionally a spiced fruit mixture encased in bread dough, but the dough gradually gave way to a lighter shortcrust pastry case and the name became simply black bun.

Serves 12–16

INGREDIENTS

For the pastry:
280g plain flour
½ tsp baking powder
grated zest and juice of
    1 lemon
150g unsalted butter,
    diced
3–4 tbsp cold water
1 medium egg, beaten to
    glaze

For the filling:
450g raisins
600g currants
100g whole almonds,
    roughly chopped
50g walnuts, roughly
    chopped
150g plain flour
75g caster or demerara
    sugar
1 tsp ground allspice
1 tsp ground ginger
1 tsp ground cinnamon
½ tsp cream of tartar
½ tsp baking powder
2 tbsp whisky
4 tbsp (approx.) milk

METHOD

1. For the pastry, sift the flour and baking powder into a bowl, then stir in the lemon zest. Rub in the butter, then add the lemon juice and 3–4 tbsp cold water – enough to bind to a stiff dough.
2. Turn out onto a lightly floured board and roll out thinly. Use two-thirds of the pastry to line a buttered, square 23cm/9in cake tin. Roll out the remaining pastry to fit as a lid, cover and chill both the lid and the case for half an hour or so.
3. Preheat the oven to 140°C/275°F/Gas 1.
4. For the filling, mix everything together, except the whisky and milk. (I do this with my hands – it is easier.) Now add the whisky, and enough milk to moisten the mixture. Turn into the pastry case and press down well.
5. Dampen the edges of the pastry all round with a little water and place the rolled-out pastry lid on top. Press together the edges to seal, then cut off any remaining pastry. Prick all over with a fork. Using a very thin skewer, prick right through to the base of the tin: 6–8 pricks altogether. Brush the surface with some beaten egg, retaining a little for later.
6. Bake for 2–2½ hours until golden brown on top, reglazing with the remaining beaten egg after 1 hour of baking.
7. Cool in the tin for at least 2 hours, then carefully decant onto a wire rack to cool completely. Wrap in foil and store in an airtight container for at least 1 month – and for anything up to 3–4 months.

Christmas Fact #8

Edinburgh's Hogmanay fireworks should last 4 hours.

Each December a crew of 14 pyrotechnists walk over 105 miles setting up the fireworks for Edinburgh's famous Hogmanay party. As church bells across Edinburgh ring midnight the impressive display begins, lasting 5 minutes. However, if each effect was fired individually, it would last over 4 hours.

King James IV introduced the first fireworks to Scotland, setting some off as part of a pageant in what is now King's Stables Road in Edinburgh in 1507.

Street Parties

Edinburgh is known as the home of the world's leading New Year festival – the famous Street Party. Every year Princes Street is closed to traffic and up to 50,000 revellers descend to see in the New Year with drinking and dancing, entertained by bands such as Runrig, Big Country, Pulp, Blondie and Kasabian.

There have been Hogmanay street celebrations in Edinburgh for hundreds of years. Originally, these took place near the Tron Kirk on the Royal Mile, but since 1993 they have typically been held on Princes Street. Today, the colourful array of live music, street performers, pipers, drummers and fairground rides are meticulously managed to ensure that all the 50,000 partygoers enjoy the Street Party experience. However, in the 1990s the Street Party was still a relatively informal affair, unticketed and open to anyone who wanted to attend. The 1996 party saw a staggering 300,000 people flock to Princes Street. The resulting crush caused widespread injuries with partygoers impaled on railings and trampled by crowds. Over 800 people were admitted to Edinburgh's Royal Infirmary A&E – 61 needed surgery, and 36 required emergency resuscitation. It was clear that the Street Party had become a victim of its own success and serious changes were quickly made to ensure that the event became the safe celebration that is so well-loved today.

The Paraffin Lamp

This is an adaptation of one of George Mackay Brown's famous Winter Tales, *written to continue the tradition of Orkney islanders gathering around their hearths on the long winter evenings to listen to stories.*

Old Thomas was a man who lived entirely in the past. He disliked all the fruits of progress that his fellow-islanders were beginning to splurge on: motor cars, wireless sets, gramophones, bakehouse bread, Edinburgh beer.

One morning the good-wives in every farm and croft turned a tap, and out gushed sparkling water, for the first time. What an improvement that was! The old man went on taking his two pails to the well on the side of Wilderfea.

'Now, Thomas, look here,' said the minister one day when he was visiting. 'This won't do at all! Your life would be very much easier if you marched with the times. Can't you see that? What's wrong with a wireless set? How fine it is to hear the news, and the weather forecast, and Scottish dance music … And that hearth over there, and the iron chain for hanging your pots and kettle on – man, Thomas, the women here are never done praising their stoves – what a change it's made in their lives … If you had running water, too, what a lot cleaner you could get your shirts, and your bedclothes and everything.'

There was silence for a while on each side of the

hearth. The old man seemed to be considering the minister's advice. He said, after a while, that the worst thing that had happened in the kirk in his time was when they started singing man-made hymns in place of the psalms of David. Could the minister not raise that matter at the next Presbytery meeting in Kirkwall?

The minister rose, and pressed the old rough rheumaticky hand, and went away with a sigh.

The next thing to go down under the march of progress was the tilley lamp. They had hissed and glared on every farm dresser for twenty winters and more. In a month or two, electricity was to come to the island. The electricians from the town had a busy time of it, wiring every house for the great switch-on. The wives bought cookers, irons, radios, toasters, fan-heaters, fires. (A few even went so far as to enquire about refrigerators.)

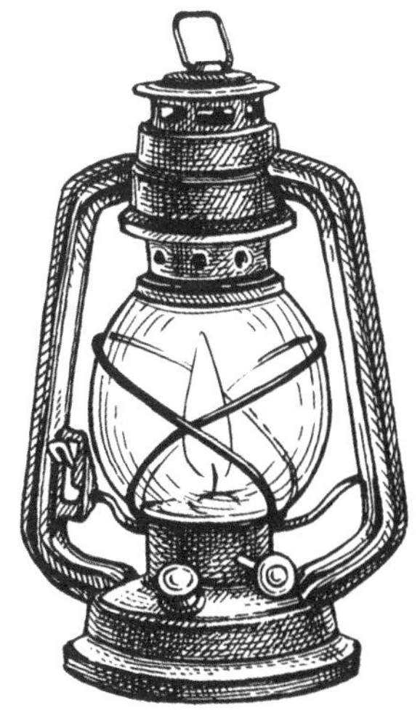

That winter the old man fell ill, with influenza or some other infection. He had been failing slowly, of course, for years. 'This is the end of him,' said the islanders. 'Poor old Thomas.' They carried him down to the pier on a stretcher and shipped him to the hospital in Kirkwall. While he was away, the minister and a few others decided that, if he was ever to come back, the old man could not go on living in the same conditions of hardship. 'We will do nothing rash,' said the minister. 'We will not overwhelm him all at once with the benefits of science. But it's time that old paraffin lamp was done away with – impossible to read by it – dangerous too, if he was to knock it over. Thomas – if he comes home – will come home to a bright electric bulb in the ceiling.'

Thomas did come home, after a month, in the depths of winter. He had fought off the illness – some of the dark power of the earth, hoarded slowly over many generations, was still in him. He thanked the islanders for all their kindness to him. He thanked them for the pear-shaped opaque thing hanging from his ceiling. So that was what electric light was like? Old Thomas switched it on – his house had never been so bright ...

That evening, when the minister went along to see how the old man was after his journey, he found him reading *The Pilgrim's Progress* by the dim light of the paraffin lamp. Thomas was very pleased to see the minister. He said that was a very handy thing, the electric light. He could see by it to fill his old lamp, and trim the wick, and light it with a wisp of straw from the fire.

A Scot walks into
a baker and asks,
'Is that a black bun
or a meringue?'

*

The baker responds,
'Naw, ye're right,
it's a black bun.'

FIRST-FOOTING IN EDINBURGH.

First-Footing

Warm hospitality has always been a traditional part of Hogmanay celebrations. For centuries Scots have welcomed strangers into their homes in the hope of encouraging good fortune in the year to come. One of the most well-known examples of this is first-footing, the practice of visiting your neighbours after the midnight bells. Traditionally, the first-footer is the first person to cross your threshold after midnight, but they must not have been present in the house before midnight. They will usually bring a gift of shortbread or black bun to fill your belly and a lump of coal to warm your fire. The first-footer will be welcomed with a dram of whisky, and kisses from all the women in the house. Tall, dark-haired men are thought to bring good luck, while women or light-haired men are considered unlucky.

Dressed Herring

First-footing on Hogmanay has many associated traditions, but the most unusual one has to be the Dundonian custom of gifting a dressed herring – quite literally, a herring in a dress. It isn't clear how or why the tradition started, but it was common practice across Dundee, Arbroath and Brechin for decades.

The fitted-out herrings could be bought from fish stalls on the Mid Kirk Style. They were often dressed as brides, or in kilts made of scraps of fabric or paper. The fancier the dress the better.

Until around the 1970s, first-footers in Dundee would cross the threshold of their neighbours after midnight on Hogmanay with the fishy gift which would then be hung in the kitchen for good luck. The tradition has largely died out perhaps due to contemporary hygiene preferences, but there are calls to revive it, albeit with model fish instead of real ones.

Open the Door

Open the door for the auld year
It is the pairtin-time:
Open the door for the new year
And lat the bairn win hame.

Bundle your winter'd joy and grief
On the back of the year that's düne:
Open your hert for the new life
And lat the bairn come in.

William Soutar

New Year's Day Steak Pie

Steak pie has long been a staple of New Year's Day for many Scots, probably because it can be bought from the local butcher or made in advance and just popped in the oven to finish off on the day itself. An easy dinner even if you're feeling a wee bit peely-wally after the night before.

INGREDIENTS
1 tbsp sunflower oil
1 large onion
2 tbsp plain flour
½ tsp salt
ground black pepper to taste
800g diced stewing steak
1 bay leaf
750ml beef stock
1 tbsp tomato puree
1 tbsp Marmite
1 tsp caster sugar
4 medium carrots, peeled and sliced
1 egg, beaten
1 sheet of ready-rolled puff pastry

METHOD

1. Preheat the oven to 180°C/350°F/Gas 4.
2. Gently fry the onions with the oil for 6–8 minutes in a large casserole.
3. Mix the flour and salt together in a large bowl. Season with black pepper.
4. Trim the beef of hard fat or sinew and cut into 3cm cubes. Toss the meat in the flour.
5. Add the floured beef to the pan with the onions. Cook for 5 minutes until the beef is browned.
6. Add the bay leaf, stock, tomato puree, Marmite and sugar. Stir well and bring to the boil. Cover and place in the oven for 2 hours.
7. Add sliced carrots and stir well. Transfer the beef mixture to a large pie dish.
8. Brush beaten egg around the edge of the pie dish and lay the puff pastry sheet on top. Brush more beaten egg all over the surface of the pastry. Make a small hole in the middle to allow steam to escape. You can now put the pie aside until you are ready to eat it.
9. On the day you want to eat the pie, place it in the oven and bake for 25–30 minutes at 200°C/400°F/Gas 6 until the pastry is puffed and golden.

New Year's Day Shinty

Shinty is Scotland's answer to hockey and is similar to Ireland's hurling. Today it is a 12-aside game played with curved sticks and tall goal posts, and it has been played in some form on New Year's Day since at least the early 1800s.

In the past these New Year's Day matches were played all over Scotland – on any flat ground that could be found between townships on Shetland, on the beaches of Lewis (where the ball was made by heating old shoes to release the glue from the soles) and even in a huge 30-aside match at Glasgow's Queen's Park, with one team in kilts and the other in knickerbockers. Players were known to partake of whisky during the games, and had a reputation for being wild and rough.

Today many of the local island games have sadly died out, but there are several formal matches including the fiercely contested Lovat Cup, played between Beauly and Lovat. There are also fixtures in Badenoch, Lochaber and Oban. There is even a Boxing Day match held on Wimbledon Common by the London Camanachd shinty club.

Loony Dook

Scots have been throwing themselves into the frigid waters of the Firth of Forth on New Year's Day long before the current enthusiasm for wild swimming caught on. The tradition was first started by three friends in South Queensferry in the 1980s and has grown to the point where thousands of people participate in the cultural phenomenon, dressed in everything from bikinis to mermaid tails and nuns' habits.

The daft event has inspired several other Loony Dooks across Scotland, including Kinghorn in Fife, Portobello in Edinburgh and North Berwick in East Lothian. Collectively the various Loony Dooks raise thousands of pounds for charities and good causes every year – and have no doubt cured a few hangovers along the way too.

What do
vampires
sing at
Hogmanay?

*

Auld fang
syne.

Saining

Saining is a Scots word for blessing or protecting. The practice of saining on New Year's Day is an ancient practice whereby people would bless their house (and sometimes their livestock) with water from a river ford believed to be crossed by both the living and the dead. They would also carry burning juniper branches through the home before opening the windows to let in the fresh air of the New Year.

Burning the Clavie

The people of Burghead in Moray burn a clavie to celebrate old New Year on 11 January. Interestingly, their stubborn adherence to the ancient Julian calendar makes it possible to date the origins of their celebrations, as they must have begun prior to 1752 when the new Gregorian calendar was adopted. This is at least 100 years earlier than we have been able to officially date any other Scottish fire festivals.

The clavie is a whisky cask that has been split in two and filled with cask staves. It is set alight and paraded through the town, followed by a crowd of revellers, until it is ceremoniously set into the Clavie Stone on the rampart of an ancient fort on Doorie Hill. As it makes its way through the streets staves of burning wood fall to the ground and onlookers scramble to retrieve them as they are said to bring good luck for the coming year.

Stovies

This cheap and filling dish originated as a weekday meal made from the leftovers of the Sunday roast but in more recent years has become a staple of Hogmanay cuisine.

Serves 4–6

INGREDIENTS
600–800g onions
100ml fat, dripping from meat or bacon, or oil
1.5kg potatoes
125ml stock, leftover gravy or water, or 1–2 tbsp
    Japanese miso
leftover meat or grilled bacon
salt
ground black pepper, grated nutmeg or ground
    allspice
2–3 tbsp chopped parsley, chives or spring onions

METHOD
1. Slice the onions thinly or put into a food processor with the slicing disc and whizz.
2. Melt fat/oil in a large sauté or frying pan with a tight-fitting lid. When hot, add onions.
3. Reduce the heat and fry until they are soft and greatly reduced. Continue to reduce and brown if preferred.

4. Slice potatoes to preferred thickness. If using floury potatoes, they can also be unevenly sliced, so that the thin ones reduce to a mush while the thick ones stay whole when cooked. Waxy potatoes which will not break up are best sliced the same size so they are all soft at the same time. They can be sliced thinly in a food processor using the slicing disc. Add to the onions and stir well.
5. Place lid on the pan and leave to cook for about 5 minutes, stirring when necessary to prevent sticking. The heat must be at its lowest possible.
6. Add water, stock or gravy from a roast to moisten and prevent sticking. The less water added the drier the stovies.
7. Cover and cook till potatoes are soft, stirring occasionally to prevent sticking.
8. Add cooked meat and mix through the stovies. Taste and season.
9. Before serving, sprinkle with a handful of finely chopped parsley, chives or spring onions

Up Helly Aa

Up Helly Aa is one of Scotland's most famous festivals. Every year, on the last Tuesday in January, over 1,000 singing guisers and musicians walk through the streets of Lerwick in Shetland in a huge torchlit procession behind a Viking galley, which is eventually set alight. There are also 11 other Up Helly Aas spread across Shetland between January and March (including one featuring the Brownie troop from the rural village of Walls). The main festival can have up to 50 squads of guisers, but only one, the Jarl Squad, is permitted to dress as Vikings.

Due to its association with Vikings, it would be easy to assume that Up Helly Aa is an ancient festival, but it actually has much more contemporary roots. The first official festival began less than 150 years ago, in 1881. It is thought to have originated from the lively Hogmanay celebrations of visiting sailors, but has gradually migrated to the end of January. It is truly a unique and bizarre Scottish celebration, and a remarkable community effort by the people of Shetland.

Handsel Monday

Handsel is the Scots word for a New Year gift. The first Monday of the New Year was traditionally known as Handsel Monday and was celebrated by rural communities in Lowland Scotland. It was similar to English Boxing Day with lairds and farmers giving bonuses or gifts to their employees. Workers would be given a day off, and could collect half a crown or a shilling from the Master's house, with a piece of cake and glass of toddy. The gifts and celebrations would continue among the workers all day, while the master and his family saw to the work. The custom was common until well into the nineteenth century and recognised above Christmas or Hogmanay as the pinnacle of the winter festivities.

The day began early, with excited children waking whole villages by kicking tin pans through the streets. There followed a breakfast of beef fat and oats and the lighting of bonfires. Young men paraded through villages with torches and horns. Singing, drinking and (inevitably) fighting, were also key components to the celebrations.

Tipsy Laird Trifle

Trifle is a traditional English dessert often associated with Christmas. A 2020 YouGov Poll revealed that 41 per cent of respondents saw trifles as the UK's all-time favourite Christmas dessert. Most English recipes call for the sponge layer to be soaked with sherry, but the Scots palate preferred whisky and so the Tipsy Laird was born.

INGREDIENTS

250g sponge fingers (or sliced sponge cake)
raspberry jam
500g raspberries
600ml ready-made custard
4 tbsp whisky or Drambuie
250ml whipping cream

METHOD

1. Spread all the sponge fingers with jam.
2. Place a layer of sponge fingers to cover the bottom of a large bowl.
3. Place half of the raspberries on top of the sponge fingers and drizzle with the whisky or Drambuie
4. Next add a thick layer of custard.
5. Whisk the cream and spoon it over the custard.
6. Decorate the top with the remaining raspberries.

Mary, Queen of Scots had the worst Christmas luck

There are probably few people who have had as much bad luck in December as Mary, Queen of Scots. Mary was born on 8 December 1542. On the 14 December her father, James V, died, making her a queen at just six days old. Mary spent only four Christmases in Scotland before being sent to France.

At the age of 18 Mary was living in France, married to Francis II. He died on 5 December 1560, leaving Catholic Mary widowed and forced to return to Protestant Scotland.

Despite the country's Protestant reserve, Mary managed to enjoy a few jovial Christmases in Scotland at Holyrood, playing games and swapping places with her ladies-in-waiting. But even these parties were overshadowed by religious division, and the Royal musicians refused to play at Mass. Mary also planned an extravagant three-day celebration of her son's baptism at Stirling Castle in December 1566. These joyful times were not to last, however, and by Christmas 1567, aged just 25, Mary had been forced to abdicate and would spend the rest of her life as the prisoner of the English queen, Elizabeth I

In 1583, the Scottish presbyterian Church banned Christmas celebrations. In order to thwart potential rebellion, Mary was twice moved on Christmas Eve, firstly, in 1584 to Tutbury Castle, and later, while

seriously ill, to Chartley Hall in 1585. She spent her final Christmas in the Tower of London in 1586 and was executed a month and a half later. During her 45 years, she spent two Christmases in mourning, and 19 imprisoned.

Christmas Fact #9

Burke and Hare had an eventful Christmas Day in 1828

William Burke and William Hare were two of Scotland's most notorious mass murderers. During an 11-month killing-spree in 1827–28 the pair killed 16 people in Edinburgh, selling the bodies as anatomy specimens for university medical students to Dr Robert Knox at Old Surgeons' Hall.

Eventually, Hare was persuaded to turn King's witness and testified against Burke in return for immunity. The trial began at 10 a.m. on Christmas Eve 1828 and ran through the day and night until 8.30 a.m. on Christmas Day. The jury took only 50 minutes to find Burke guilty.

William Burke was executed on 28 January 1829. As further punishment for his crimes he was publicly dissected. A pocketbook made from his skin is still on display at Surgeons' Hall Museums, Edinburgh.

Nettle Burning

The young people of Orkney used to have a peculiar addition to the first-footing tradition on New Year's Day. In the weeks prior to Hogmanay, patches of nettles would be sought out, and their locations kept a closely guarded secret. Come the first of January the youths of the island would gather bunches of the fresh nettles and run around attacking people, stinging them on their hands and feet (faces were out of bounds).

A particularly dirty trick was to sneak into someone's bedroom and tuck fresh nettles under the blankets at the foot of their bed while they were sleeping. The oblivious target would wake on New Year's Day, yawn and stretch, and their feet would brush the stinging leaves – a very unpleasant way to start the year!

Montrose John and the Christmas Tree

This is the story of Montrose John, a local hooligan from the Angus town of Montrose, who one Hogmanay decided to climb the town Christmas tree. It was told by Richard Clark at the Girvan Folk Festival Storytelling Competition in 1989.

It was just the last new year but three
I climbed up the Christmas Tree
The polis wis there an they cannae tak a laugh
So I climbed oot the tree an' I buggered aff
Well I ran doon streets and I ran doon lanes
I ran up closes an' back again
I ended up at the harbour bar and I thought to hide –
    but whar?
Well I looked at the river and I thought of ma sins
I thought, 'Well, the only way oot is in.'
So I jumped in the water and swam for the bank
But the mair I swam the mair I sank
So I let maself get carried oot to sea
When I looked at the lighthouse I thought I'd deid
So I started to swim and I made for the beach
Well the tide was wi' me, so it was soon within reach
Noo you ken me, and a mean whit I say
An' am no saying I'd dae that everyday
But when ma feet hit that beach it wis an affy fine
    feelin'!

Fordyce Mortar Stane

The Aberdeenshire town of Fordyce had a unique Yule tradition featuring an ancient stone known as the Mortar Stane. A letter sent to *The Scotsman* newspaper by 'R.F.' in 1920 describes the custom:

Every year at Yuletide, the young men gather and deposit the old freestone at the door of one of the maidens of the village, selected by a vote, and it sits there till next Yuletide. Its virtue is to bring marriage to the maiden during the year.

The ceremony is old, beyond the memory of the oldest inhabitants, and is still regularly observed. As a scholar, I have participated in the scenes, which I must confess were very rough and noisy – the stone being conveyed in a farm cart, conscripted for the occasion, and pulled by scores of young men. Generally a fiddler was placed on the stone in the cart and made music for the crowd. Fiddler, fiddle and the stone were simultaneously dumped down at the door of the selected house. After the ceremony was complete, the cart was taken to the top of a steep brae and sent down into the burn, where the unhappy owner could find it the next day. I am informed now that the ceremony is carried through, at the sight of the village constable, with more decorum.

Drinking Alcohol

Pished, shwallied, blootered, buckled – the Scots have nearly as many words for being drunk as they do for snow. We have a distinguished reputation for enjoying a dram, and today Hogmanay in particular is synonymous with drinking.

Drinking traditions have varied over the centuries. The temperance movement gained traction in Scotland around 1830. It led to a banning of alcohol across many areas, creating 'dry' towns such as Kilsyth, Kirkintilloch, Wick and Lerwick. The legacy of this movement lasted for decades: Kilmacolm in Inverclyde was 'dry' for over 70 years until a pub finally opened in 1998.

For most Scots, however, heavy drinking was the norm at New Year. Traditionally, many people waited until midnight before taking a drink. Until the 19th century, it was common for people to share a Wassail bowl (consisting of warm, spiced and sweetened ale and spirits) after the midnight bells. Everyone in the household would take turns drinking from the bowl and it would then be taken round all the neighbours. The practice came to a sudden end in Edinburgh in 1812 when a group of hooligans

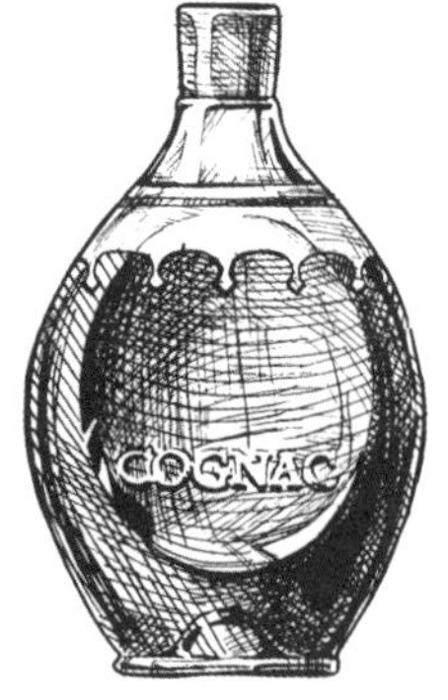

roamed the streets on Hogmanay brutally mugging intoxicated Wassailers. The horrific attacks resulted in the deaths of a policeman and a young clerk, and the three perpetrators were eventually executed.

Hogmanay celebrations invariably lead to New Year's Day hangovers. Journalist Alan Taylor described the aftermath of Hogmanay in the *Scotland on Sunday* newspaper on 1 January 1990:

On the first day of the New Year the high street felt as if Armageddon had arrived. In the early afternoon men with complexions like over-milked scrambled egg went walkabout while the womenfolk prepared steak pies and defrosted peas ... It was a communal commiseration, that peculiar macho Scottish phenomenon of sharing and wallowing in a hangover.

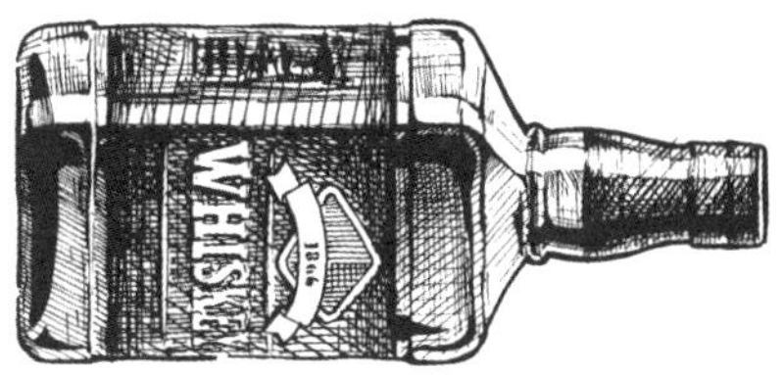

The Man Who Kicked the Bone at Hogmanay

This story comes from the traveller community in Rossshire. The motif of reanimated bones is common in many biblical texts, and the significance of the crossed bannocks suggests a Christian influence in the tale.

Once in the Highlands of Scotland a man moved to a croft on the outskirts of a village. He lived there with a housekeeper as he was not married. The man found that the people of the village were not welcoming to him, so he asked his housekeeper for advice. She told him that there was to be a funeral for one of the villagers the next day and suggested that he should attend to pay his respects.

The following day was Hogmanay and the man dutifully walked to the church to attend the funeral. At the end of the service all the villagers were chatting and inviting each other for Hogmanay that evening – but nobody spoke to the newcomer.

Disheartened and lonely, the man started to walk home. As he walked he came across a bone by the side of the path. Angry at the villagers, he kicked the bone into the grass and said 'No one is inviting me to Hogmanay, I may as well invite you!'

On New Year's Day the man's housekeeper called him to tell him that there was an old man walking towards the croft. Neither the crofter nor the housekeeper knew the man, but Scottish hospitality dictated that they welcome him into the house. The crofter gave the old man a dram of whisky while the housekeeper finished preparing the New Year's Day feast and laid the table.

As soon as the food was placed upon the table it disappeared, not a single crumb was left. The crofter looked at the old man who was wiping his mouth and called for more food. Again, the minute the food touched the table it vanished, and again the old man wiped his mouth. The crofter bid the housekeeper to make some bannocks and mark them with a cross. When she placed these upon the table the old man remarked that he was full and must be on his way. He invited the crofter to walk with him a while. Not wanting to appear rude the crofter agreed and as they walked he asked the old man why he had come.

'When you invite me I always come.'

Confused the crofter continued down the road a while before telling the old man that he must head back. As he turned towards his croft he saw that it had disappeared. In its place was only a grassy knoll.

'How has this happened? We've only been walking for a few minutes?' he asked the old man.

'You have been a long time wi' me,' said the old man. 'There's nobody in this place now that will know you.'

The crofter began his walk back to where the croft had stood. With each step he became more stooped, his eyesight faded, and he became deaf. His clothes fell into tatters and his beard grew grey and long.

The villagers could not explain the sudden appearance of this very ancient man. Finally, the oldest man in the parish remembered his grandfather telling a story from his father of a newcomer to the village who had disappeared with a stranger on Hogmanay. Before the villagers could question the ancient man he passed away, and they never learned the truth of the man who kicked the bone at Hogmanay.

Christmas Fact #10

The people of Inverness once ate whale meat for Christmas Dinner

On 18 December 1851 there was great excitement among the residents of Inverness as a whale became trapped within the narrows of Kessock Ferry, a stretch of water across the strait between the Moray and Beauly Firths. The poor creature became stranded on Christmas Day and was swiftly plundered for its meat by local fishermen. Many Inverness families had a large helping of whale meat added to their Christmas dinner that year.

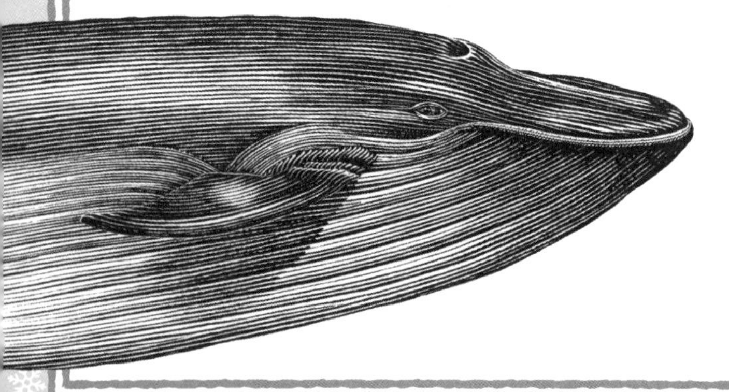

Auld Lang Syne

No book about Scotland's Christmas and Hogmanay traditions would be complete without mention of Robert Burns' most famous song, 'Auld Lang Syne'. It is recognised by Guiness World Records as the third most frequently sung song in the English language (only beaten by 'Happy Birthday' and 'For He's a Jolly Good Fellow').

Burns claimed to have heard it being sung by an old man in 1788, and dutifully wrote it down. It has since become synonymous with New Year's Eve across the world. It is usually shortened to just the first and last verses.

> Should auld acquaintance be forgot,
> And never brought to mind?
> Should auld acquaintance be forgot,
> And auld lang syne?
>
> (*Chorus*)
> For auld lang syne, my jo,
> For auld lang syne,
> We'll tak a cup o' kindness yet,
> For auld lang syne.
>
> And surely ye'll be your pint-stowp!
> And surely I'll be mine!
> And we'll tak a cup o' kindness yet,
> For auld lang syne.

Should auld ac-quain-tance be for-got, and ne - ver brought to

mind? Should auld ac-quain-tance be for-got, And auld lang

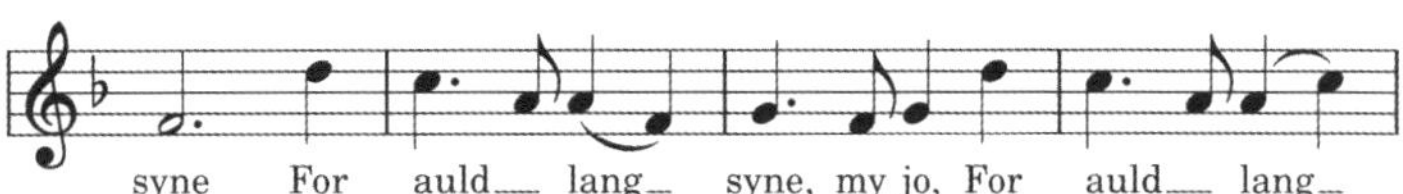
syne For auld lang syne, my jo, For auld lang

syne. We'll tak a cup of kind-ness yet, For auld lang syne.

We twa hae run about the braes
And pou'd the gowans fine;
But we've wander'd mony a weary fitt
Sin auld lang syne.

We twa hae paidl'd in the burn,
Frae mornin' sun till dine;
But seas between us braid hae roar'd
Sin auld lang syne.

And there's a hand, my trusty fiere!
And gie's a hand o' thine!
And we'll tak a right gud-willie-waught,
For auld lang syne.

Robert Burns

Acknowledgements

Many thanks to all who have helped during the course of researching and writing this book. It is impossible to list them all, but I'm especially grateful to family and friends, the team at Birlinn, Sue Lawrence, Rosemary Goring and Alan Taylor.

Picture credits
Alamy Stock Photo: pp. 10, 25, 39, 40, 48–9, 61, 62, 73, 82, 104, 117, 119, 123, 127; iStock: pp. 17, 19, 21, 26, 31, 44, 46, 54, 65, 70, 78–9, 85, 107, 110, 121, 129, 131, 132, 133, 136, 137, 140, 143; National Trust for Scotland: 91

Text credits
pp. 50–1 'How I'll Decorate My Tree', by Liz Lochhead from
    A Handsel (Polygon, 2023), reproduced by permission of
    Polygon © Liz Lochhead
pp. 52–4 Yule Log recipe by kind permission of Sue Lawrence
    © Sue Lawrence
pp. 63–4 Cock-a-leekie Soup recipe from *The 44 Scotland Street
    Cookbook* by Anna Marshall (Polygon, 2023), reproduced by
    kind permission of the author and Polygon © Anna Marshall
pp.74–5 Cloutie Dumpling recipe from *Scottish Cookery* by
    Catherine Brown © the estate of Catherine Brown
p. 84 Excerpt from 'Winter' from *In a Time of Distance* by
    Alexander McCall Smith (Polygon, 2020), reproduced by kind
    permission of the author and Polygon © Alexander McCall
    Smith
pp. 86–7 Petticoat Tails Shortbread recipe from *New Scottish
    Baking* by Sue Lawrence (Birlinn, 2024), reproduced by kind
    permission of the author and Birlinn © Sue Lawrence
pp. 101–02 Black Bun recipe from *New Scottish Baking* by Sue
    Lawrence (Birlinn, 2024), reproduced by kind permission of the
    author and Birlinn © Sue Lawrence
pp.106–08 'The Paraffin Lamp' adapted from *Winter Tales* by
    George Mackay Brown (John Murray, 1995) © and reproduced
    by permission of the Estate of George Mackay Brown
pp. 124–5 Stovies recipe adapted from *Scottish Cookery* by
    Catherine Brown (Birlinn, 2013), reproduced by permission of
    Birlinn © the Estate of Catherine Brown
p. 134 Montrose John and the Christmas Tree, as told by Richard
    Clark: https://www.tobarandualchais.co.uk/track/90843?l=en